CHRISTIAN PHRENOLOGY

CHRISTIAN PHRENOLOGY

JOSEPH BUNNEY

9 789356 140011
ISBN: 978-93-5614-001-1

Published: 1839

LECTOR HOUSE

LECTOR HOUSE LLP
E-MAIL: lectorpublishing@gmail.com

CHRISTIAN PHRENOLOGY,
A GUIDE TO SELF-KNOWLEDGE.

BY

JOSEPH BUNNEY

ΓΝΩΘΙ ΣΕΑΥΤΟΝ.

SECOND EDITION

MDCCCXXXIX.

CONTENTS

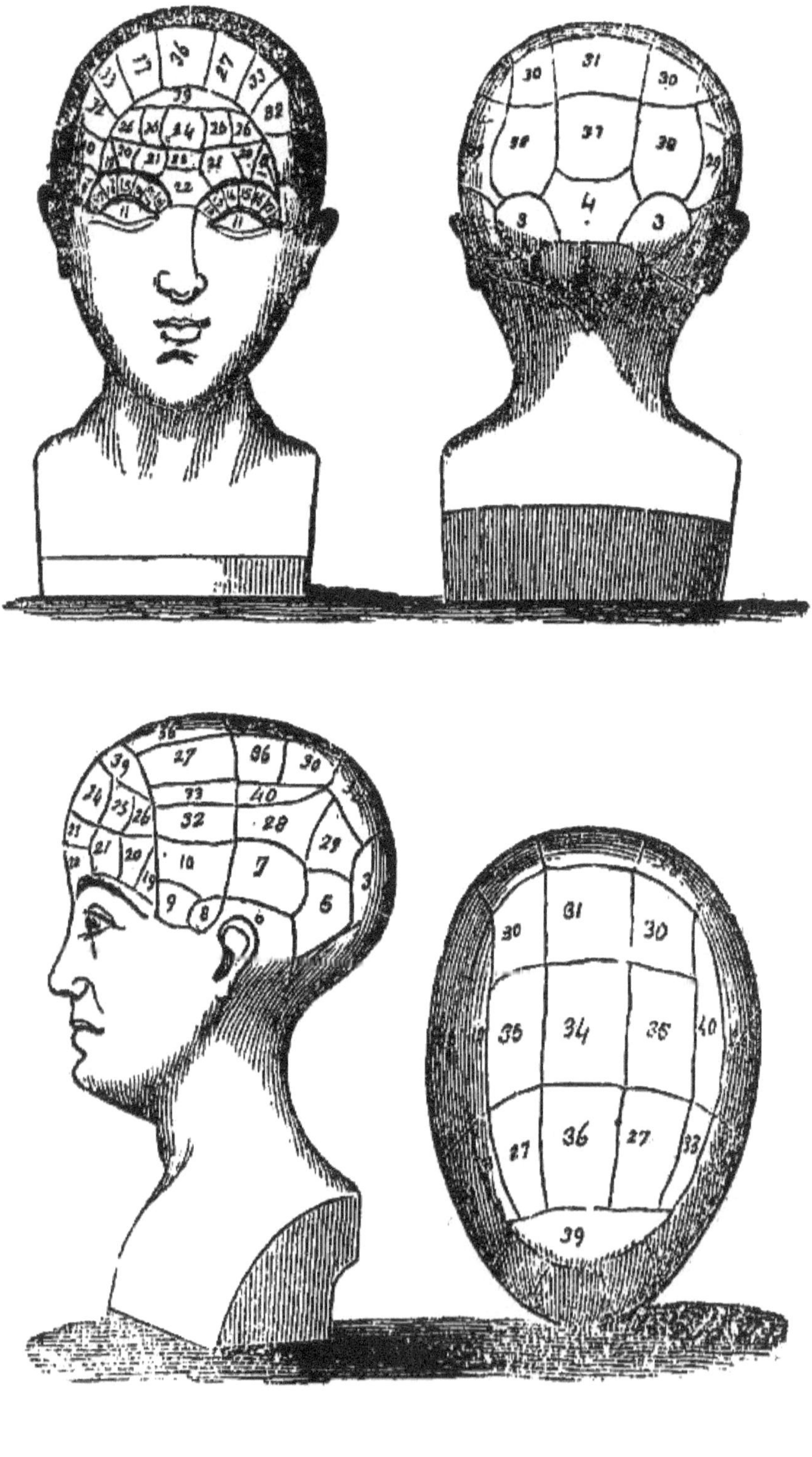

30
31
30
38
37
38
29
3
4
3
39
27
36
30
24
25
26
33
40
32
28
21
20
29
10
7
19
9
8
6
3
30
31
30
35
34
35
40
27
36
27
33
39

INTRODUCTION TO THE STUDY OF PHRENOLOGY.

Phrenology is a system of Mental Philosophy. It enquires into the quality and condition of the mind, estimating the faculties, sentiments, and propensities of the individual, without being deceived by personal esteem or the voice of partial praise; for as it too frequently occurs that minds of the highest order are more or less under the influence of self love, or a desire for the admiration of others, so are they blinded to their own weaknesses and in some measure rendered incapable of acknowledging their faults even to themselves. This defect, a defect of the race rather than of the individual, presents an effectual barrier to all mental improvement, for minds however highly gifted are always in some measure led astray by self gratulation or the flattering commendations of others, and thus they are led to overlook their own errors, or to congratulate themselves that they are not as other men are, and the mental eye becomes blinded to what is wrong in its own intellectual organization although sensitively awake to the erroneous feelings and propensities of others. It is the province of PHRENOLOGY to measure the external features of the mind's agent, and to facilitate the study of MAN without diverging into metaphysical error on the one hand, or materialism on the other.

Phrenology then is one of those beautiful revelations of applicable science which could only have been made known in an æra of intellectual cultivation. It is in accordance with man's advancement in civilization and refinement.—It was not needed in the days of

"High emprise or priestly power."

for when men were measured by their prowess, and when might was right, a standard of intellect would have been of little value; but amidst the discoveries of the 19th century it comes to us as a monitor and a friend; Its developement forms a striking fact in the philosophy of history—for as we trace the long and varied records of physical discovery from the time of Archimedes to the coronation of Victoria,—we invariably find that whatever science, or whatever art has been made known to us, it has always been the forerunner of new chapters in the history of man: thus Astronomy led the way to magnetism—Magnetism led to the scientific principles of navigation,—and the steam engine, mighty as its power appears, is but in accordance with the advanced wants of mankind; and so with every other instance, in proportion to the discoveries of intellect, has man advanced in the scale of intelligence and humanity,—with mind, so has matter progressed, until from the unlettered savage, he has arrived at the gates of that scientific temple whose lessons teach him, that now, having laid out the earth for his sustenance, peopled the ocean with his race, and proved his mastery over all things, it is time that he should arise and conquer self,—

> Know then thyself, and seek not God to scan,
> The proper study of mankind is man! Pope.

To do this, man must be studied in his moral, social, and religious condition; thus only is he enabled to gratify that inward yearning after what is great and good which is the basis of all improvement. It is necessary however to learn what is imperfect before improvement can be attempted. We must learn our own mental constitution and compare it with a standard of excellence, and what standard can we have, but that all surpassing goodness that created man in his own image? HE in whom even Pilate found no fault—who said "I am the vine, and ye are the branches,"—who went about doing good, and who said to his disciples, "Be ye therefore perfect, even as your father which is in heaven is perfect." This is the standard that we should look up to—to the Author of all good;—to His life upon earth as the line of our conduct here—to his sufferings in our day of tribulation—to His glory as the end that we would one day share in.

Such is the object that forces itself upon the mind, when liberated from the baser passions of humanity, the spirit can indulge in its own lofty aspirations—it feels a noble elevation of purpose in contemplating the improvement of its being—and it feels capable of following out a design so beautiful,—there is a dimly revealed pleasure in devoting every energy to the acquisition of an end so glorious, and the pleasure is pure, elevated, and ennobling, it is neither transient nor violent, but it seems to be breathed into the heart, making it wiser, better, and happier—It is not the pleasure that we have sought for in life, but the calm and quiet enjoyment that is referred to the mind, as the seat of all pure and rational delight: and to the brain, as a pleasure that will endure and increase, and fade not away like the momentary intoxications of animal delight: the pleasure of a good object is referrible to the mind, and to the brain as the seat of that mind, and we ask, Is the mind the offspring of that brain? or, Is the brain the organ through which the mind acts? a moment's thought answers the question; in a few short years that brain will be mouldering away in the silent tomb, whilst the mind that animated it, can never die; thus then we arrive at the seat of the mind, a fact universally allowed by all philosophers, in all places, and at all times, and by reasoning upon this simple fact, we are led through progressive stages of induction, until we have arrived at a knowledge of that most valuable but most difficultly exercised faculty, Self-control.

Now, we know well that the eye and the ear receive their faculties from the brain, through the medium of the nerves. Thus, the eye may be delighted by gazing on an extended view of nature; the ear by listening to the sublime cadences of sacred music; but if we sever the delicate filament that conveys the sense of enjoyment to the brain, as the seat of all pleasure, resulting from the exercise of the eye or the ear, so do we immediately sever the sentient being from the perception of beauty in form or landscape, or of harmony in sound. So it is with a limb, if we divide the fibre or nerve connecting the muscles of that limb with the brain, we immediately deprive the organ of feeling and volition. Thus, then, the feelings, the senses, and the enjoyments are referred to the brain as the seat of the mind, and it would be as irrational to suppose that the brain in its entirety is influenced by every sensation, perception, or impulse, as to suppose that the whole body is required for an operation affecting only a part: so by analogy we learn, that as the eye is given us to see with, the ear to hear with, the tongue to speak with; when neither eye, ear, or tongue is adapted to any other use, so, in like manner we are led to infer, that particular parts of the brain are endowed with powers, peculiar to themselves; for it would be equally rational to suppose that a man could in some measure read with the ear, smell with the eye, or see with the nose, as to assert that the same portion of brain could be directed by the mind at will, to study poetry, or sculpture, the arts of money getting, or direct to the enjoyments of love. Such operations of the mind are essentially different; the poet, the sculptor, the man of this world, and the lover of pleasure have portions of the brain, individually adapted to the various operations of the mind, and as the mind is developed by natural circumstances, by hereditary prejudices,—the effects of early training,—the results of education,—the influence of good or bad example, or the untoward events that occur in life,—so is the effect of each and every one of these duly registered upon the mind, and upon the brain, as the organ of that mind, so that at any and every period of existence an external examination of the brain points out what propensities, sentiments, and faculties are at that period in existence, and as a due cultivation or improper neglect of the mental powers is invariably recorded through the mind itself acting upon the brain with more or less energy in those individual parts most generally exercised, so does Phrenology—the science of the brain, as an unbiassed friend, point out what errors of the imagination are to be shunned—what propensities to be conquered, what faculties to be cultivated, what sentiments to be given up. So does it present itself as a means whereby we may know our own weaknesses and conquer them—our strength, and be enabled to exert it. So does it point out whatever may be predominant in our nature for good or for evil, teaching us by a monitor far more true than even the heart itself, how to remedy our faults in this life, and gradually by severe and constant practice, teaching us how to become more fitted for the life to come.

HISTORICAL ACCOUNT OF PHRENOLOGY.

In examining the history, or the progress of discovery in any particular science, we are irresistibly led to enquire *why* a series of facts like those which constitute its basis should have remained so long hidden from the eye of man. We know that the doctrines we are investigating are founded upon facts, and if those facts are in operation at this moment, they must have been equally so a thousand years ago, or our enquiries cannot be based upon Truth, since Truth is eternal. If, then, in perusing the records of phrenology, we are led to wonder at the long ages of human ignorance, Are we not equally surprised that all physical science should have existed so many ages, without the cognizance of man? Do we not wonder that thousands of years floated down the stream of Time, before man discovered *why* the lightning flashed across the heavens, or *why* the needle pointed to the pole, and are we not even now unable to tell *why* the polar Aurora diffuses its ethereal light? Why then single out Phrenology for disbelief, because it is new, is gold the less gold because fresh from the mine? or truth less true because recently revealed? *We* cannot tell why phrenology has so long remained unknown, but we may refer the reason to the wisdom of that Almighty Intelligence who placed his bow in the heavens, and fashioned that wonderful cycle of events that in every age has been suited to the wants and capacities of man. Phrenology could not have existed in any age but one wherein mind had asserted its mastery over matter, and although the understanding was in some measure prepared for the reception of new truths by the physiognomy of Lavater, and the facial line introduced by Camper, yet experience proved that Lavater's theories were not generally applicable, and the means proposed by Campor at the best times uncertain. Anatomists and physiologists toiled at discovering the seat of the mind, they dissected and drew conclusions—but so vague and unsatisfactory was the knowledge communicated, that the more the anatomist dissected, the more he became entangled in a mass of conjecture and perplexity. The metaphysician failed too; he studied the mind chiefly through himself and by recording his own knowledge of his faculties, was led into error: like the nautilus he retreated into his own shell and thus sought to learn what was without, and as may be supposed men of different minds arrived at different results:—such was the state of mental knowledge about 1760. The method pursued by Dr. Gall, was essentially different; at an early period he was led to notice the difference of talents and disposition in his schoolmates and companions, he found one with a retentive memory, another with a talent for languages, one was remarkable for elegance of style, another for dullness, and a third for close reasoning; he found their dispositions equally different, and this diversity appeared to regulate their partialities and aversions; some showed a liking for play, others for books, and a third class for mechanical handiwork. In this manner every one presented an individual character; some years after he found that persons with a great talent for learning by heart were those with whom it was most difficult for him to compete, and he noticed that all these had prominent eyes, he then recollected that his early companions had the same feature prominent, and when he entered the University he directed his attention to this fact, and found that all those who had prominent eyes possessed a great facility of learning by heart, even in cases where they possessed no particular talent. Although this connexion between talent and external appearance was not sufficiently established to be considered as a *certain* circumstance, Dr. Gall could not divest himself of a belief in the relationship of the one fact to the other, and after much reflection he conceived that if memory for words had an external indication, the same circumstance might be traced to the other intellectual powers; looking therefore only at general indications he believed he could trace the existence of talents for painting, music and mechanics, he marked also the external features of individuals possessing great determination of character, this suggested to him the idea of looking to the head for all the moral sentiments, referring the state of the skull to the influence of the Brain.

Here then commenced the difficulties which appeared as soon as Dr. Gall compared his own observations from nature, with the opinions of Physiologists and Metaphysicians; he found that while some placed the sentient soul or intellectual faculties in the brain, others placed it in the heart, or the cerebellum, or even in the viscera, so that he hesitated about the correctness of his conclusions, he observed also that the principal difference of mental faculty was not owing to difference of education or accidental circumstances,—if the difference were accidental, the project he now contemplated would be hopeless, but he recollected that his brothers, and sisters, and schoolfellows had all received a similar education and equal care, yet many upon whom the teachers had bestowed great attention were still far behind their companions.

> "Often," says Dr. GALL, "we were accused of want of will, or deficiency in zeal; but many of us could not, even with the most ardent desire, followed out by the most obstinate efforts, attain, in some pursuits, even to mediocrity; while in some other points, some of us surpassed our schoolfellows without an effort, and almost, it might be said, without perceiving it ourselves. But, in point of fact, our masters did not appear to attach much faith to the system which taught equality of mental faculties: for they thought themselves entitled to exact more from one scholar, and less from another. They spoke frequently of natural gifts, or of the gifts of God, and consoled their pupils in the words of the Gospel, by assuring them that each would be required to render an account, only in proportion to the gifts he had received."

Convinced by this, that there is a diversity of talent and of disposition, he encountered another obstacle in the conventional terms used to express the actions of the mind. Metaphysicians spoke of judgment, perception, thought, memory and imagination, but Gall wished to express a faculty for music, for painting and for mechanics, he therefore abandoned the theories and opinions of others resolving to learn by direct observation from nature; he visited prisons, schools and lunatic asylums, was introduced to courts, to colleges and the seats of justice; and wherever he heard of persons distinguished for any particular endowment or deficiency, he observed and studied the external features of those particular heads. In this manner by degrees of induction he felt himself warranted in his belief that the configurations of the head indicate the mental powers; in addition to this examination during life, whenever any of the persons died with whose peculiarities he had become acquainted during life, he used every means to be allowed to examine their brain after death, and thus he succeeded in arriving at the first outlines of those facts which time afterwards developed. In these researches he found that the brain covered by the *dura mater* presented a form exactly corresponding to that which the skull had exhibited during life: and being confident in the correctness of his system he announced it to the world at Vienna, in 1796. The successive steps that he passed over, were, 1. He observed the relationship between particular talents and particular forms of the head. 2. He ascertained that the figure and size of the brain corresponded in every point with the skull. 3. He dissected the brain minutely so as to investigate its structure.

Dr. Spurzheim studied under Gall, in 1800, and in 1804 became associated with him in his labours; since that period many new and valuable discoveries were made by them in the anatomy and physiology of the brain; the truths thus elucidated mere formed into a system of mental philosophy.

It was impossible to foresee what results would follow the exposition of this doctrine. Dr. Gall's mode of enquiry was plain and simple; thus he found that a desire for gain bore relation to the size of one part of the brain—he called it the organ of *theft*, because he found it largest in thieves; the propensity to destroy, he called *murder*, because he found it largest in individuals condemned for that crime—in like manner benevolence and other organs, for as Dr. Gall had not laid out any arrangement, a series of disjointed facts was all that could be arrived at, leaving their value to be determined at a future period, when the multitude of facts should require some arrangement. As soon, therefore, as the value of the materials had been ascertained by time and further investigation, the eye of philosophy at once detected the materials for a system of mental elucidation, and phrenological facts were arranged into a scientific system, whose importance has been universally recognized: facts that had hitherto appeared isolated were soon connected with others and the obloquy that had been thrown upon it by public ridicule, was overpowered by the presence of truth. The doctrines which at first were a rude and undigested mass of unconnected facts, whose apparent results were neither promising nor inviting, now became changed in character,—it was recognized to be the science of mind and its value was apparent, the new opinions had been doubted, simply because they were new, but they bore upon them the impress of truth: those who were adverse to its doctrines, were those who had not studied its principles; and those who doubt it now are those who have never examined the volume of nature, from which the page of science has been torn. Those who consider its relative bearing, both upon individuals and the human race, will be convinced that Phrenology carries in its train the most valuable assistance in furthering the cause of education, morality, and religion. We cannot conclude this chapter better than by quoting the annexed extract by a popular writer from the Foreign Quarterly Review;—

> "Nothing that ever was devised by man has put in his hands so powerful an instrument to know himself, as that which we (phrenologists) have given him; for, if he believes in us, he cannot deny the evidence of his own organization. The first key to unlock the hearts of others is that which opens our own; and to know whether we judge our neighbour fairly or not, we should measure the quantity of our own feelings which we mix up in the judgment. But from this acquaintance with ourselves and others may result the greatest benefit that could accrue to social intercourse, mutual indulgence. When we recollect that each has his own particular organization, as we have ours; that it is not easy to controul the dispositions which nature has thus implanted in our minds; that we have defects as insupportable, perhaps, as any that we encounter, we shall be more disposed to bear with others' foibles, that they may pardon ours; and mutual necessity will make us tolerant.
>
> "A still higher function of phrenology, as it relates to mankind at large, not merely to the few unfortunates who labour under malady, is its empire over education. The vast error, that men are alike fitted for all professions, that all can turn their mental powers to the same account and profit, has done much injury to the education of individuals, and consequently to the general progress of the world. But our science (continue Drs. Gall and Spurzheim) shows that all men are not alike fitted for all purposes; that, in one, a receptiveness for musical, in another for mathematical instruction predominates; that some are endowed with the power of prompt perception, and others with that of abstruse induction; in short, that every walk of social life has its destined votaries. Now, it is to be hoped, that when parents have the authority of phrenology for the talents and disposition of their children, they will cultivate those which nature has made the most salient in their cranium, and not torment them with studies for which they have no sufficient organ. Should one of their boys, in defiance of birch-rods and ferulas, neglect his vocabulary to carve his taw, or cut out waggon-wheels with his penknife, let them consult one of us, and we will tell them that all the betula of Windsor forest will not make a scholar of him; we will show that, not being one of the ox-eyed, he can but ill remember words, but that having a fulness in the frontal bone just above the spheno-temporal suture, he may become an expert mechanic, an engineer, a mill-wright, or a Watt; that it is in vain to thrust in through the gluteus maximus what

cannot penetrate the head; and that flog him as they may, his *propria quæ maribus* will always be covered with chips and chisels. In the same manner we will teach them to oppose the bad propensities of youth, by withholding aliment from self-love, from obstinacy, from cruelty, and by cherishing benevolence, justice, piety; and correcting levity by gently stimulating the reflecting faculties. We can tell, too, why many a school-boy, who has carried away prizes and rewards, sinks into an ordinary adult; and why more than one dunce has burst out like a luminary in later years; for we can show the organs which make a brilliant infant and a dull man, and those which are of little use at Eton, but most essential to a statesman or a philosopher. Neither shall we allow ourselves to be imposed upon by any urchin's cunning, or mistake ill will and idleness for inability. The marks by which we judge are registered by nature, indelible, immutable, and clear to every eye.

"But individual education is a very small portion of the good which we aspire to teach—(these people really are mad; their ambition is unbounded!). We will educate nations; and nothing can prevent us from fulfilling this mission, but the destruction of the human race. We will tell the men of every country their faults and their vices, their virtues and their talents, and hold them up as clearly as size and form can be held up, to the notice of mankind. None shall escape us. Already, not only Europeans,—English, French, Germans, Italians,—the most enlightened, the most refined of men, have we scrutinized, but Asiatics under every latitude, Africans thirsting on both sides of the Equator, Americans as wild as Africans, as civilized as Europeans. We have told truths to all, and pointed out the means of improvement. At this moment, indeed, they may not listen to us, but the day will come when they will advance but by us. To us is given to decide the great question of original national propensities, as of individual propensities, and to show how they may be expanded or repressed. We shall instruct rulers how to govern, and subjects how to submit, and strike the just balance—as various as the races and the regions of the earth—between the sovereign and the people; and the first time that we inspire oppressed reason to demand her rights, and to demand no more—that we teach men how much liberty they can bear, how much privation they must yet endure, we shall have our full reward.

"So much for the practical pretensions of our science. The reader must now hear our claims to speculative superiority. Dr. Spurzheim has said, and been most heartily abused for saying—and, if the science be false, most heartily deserves to be abused for saying,—that the whole philosophy of the mind must be entirely changed; that the study of man in this respect will become a new study, &c. In this dictum—most noble or most arrogant, according to events—we (phrenologists) concur, with the loudest cheers; and in this, do we say, lies the stupendous monument of our science. Since the earliest records of philosophy, sages have speculated on the heart, the mind, the passions, and the understanding. For more than three thousand years systems have flashed, and disappeared without leaving a trace. Some of these, indeed, were abundantly ingenious; but were defective in that which alone can make them lasting, truth. It would be curious to examine the hypotheses which have grown up, one after the other, in the fertile soil of fancy, Arabian, Chinese, Persian, Egyptian, Greek, Roman, and modern European, and to see how specious and how futile all have been. Not one of them was founded on any thing but conjecture; and, until Gall appeared, it was not supposed that mental philosophy, that psychology, ever could have any other basis. But Gall proceeded entirely upon fact; and those who accuse his system as imaginative, will probably call the 'Faerie Queene' an historical poem, and 'Lear' an algebraical tragedy. He stalked from brain to brain, from organ to organ, and trampled conjecture under foot. 'The man of skulls'—aye, Mr. Edinburgh Reviewer, the *boy* of skulls—endowed in truth, with not less imagination than his predecessors, had yet more love of fact than they had; and this single faculty has placed him above them all. It is, indeed, most wonderous, that the catalogue of the innate faculties of man should have escaped the grey-haired philosophers of every age and climate, and that its first-fold should have been opened to a child of nine years old, who in maturity unrolled it all, except a leaf or two, which he left to his followers. Such a discovery, had it been made by a man after so long concealment, and so many attempts to accomplish it, would have been wonderful; but let it never be forgotten that it was the work, and not the accidental work, of an infant."

ADVANTAGES AND OBJECTS OF PHRENOLOGY.

* * * * *

> "In proportion as any branch of study leads to important and useful results—in proportion as it tends to overthrow prevailing errors—in the same degree it may be expected to call forth angry declamation from those who are trying to despise what they will not *learn*, and wedded to *prejudices* which they *cannot defend*."—ARCHBISHOP WHATELY.

* * * * *

Having pointed out in the introductory chapter the great end and aim of all learning—THE ADVANCEMENT OF MANKIND IN RELIGION, MORALITY, AND VIRTUE, we shall proceed to point out the advantages of Phrenology, in enabling man to become wiser, better, and happier. It will be universally conceded, that this life is a state of probation, that if we do well—that is, if we become God's people, we shall enter into the kingdom of heaven; but if we do evil, we shall have our portion in the lake which burneth with everlasting fire; for this reason St. Paul exhorts us to press forward to the prize of our high calling. "Let us go on unto perfection," says he, and again, "let us lay aside every weight, and the sin which doth so easily beset us"—and in another place he tells us, that "it is appointed unto men once to die, and after that the judgment."

Such then, being our situation, how imperative is the command to, "cease to do evil, and learn to do well." We must first learn what is imperfect and then strive to improve,—we must look upon SELF IMPROVEMENT, as something possible, something allied to the better portion of human nature, something worthy of the noblest care and the mightiest efforts that human beings, aiming at perfection, can even hope to aspire to. We must recall the past, watch over the present, and strengthen ourselves against the future,—we must learn what we *are* and what we *may be*, for we have in ourselves the power of controlling as well as of watching our passions and our energies, and it is this prerogative that causes human responsibility. Phrenology teaches us that mental energy is invariably accompanied by an increase of the brain, in the portion which is acted on by that energy; if the intellect be expanded, the perceptive faculties in active operation, the nobler energies of charity and veneration employed for good, it is at once apparent; so too with the baser passions, the sensualist, the ignorant, and the depraved alike reveal by their organization the spirit that moves within them, and as we know by endless facts that the brain alters in proportion to the use or disuse of faculties, sentiments, or passions; so if we are right-minded we must infer that God created no such master-piece of unerring workmanship without designing it for our good; and if so, how culpable, how criminal must they be, who dare to doubt the hand of a nobler being in a design so beautiful,—how culpable must they be who neglect to use the means laid down for their advancement,—how criminal, when they know, yet slight or scorn to employ it? But it may be asked, how can the brain enlarge or decrease by the action of the mind? Can an invisible, immaterial principle enlarge or lessen the organ through which it operates? most certainly it can,—what but *use* developes the muscular system—what but the amount of exertion makes the right arm of the gold beater nearly twice the size of his left? or why does active exertion give strength and tone to the limbs, whilst indolence renders them effeminate and small,—and if any one doubt the parallel, they cannot have examined and enquired for truth, on which alone enquiry can be based. Muscular power, considered abstractedly, is to the full as invisible and deep seated as the powers of the mind,—the mind must first direct the motions of animal power through the medium of the nerves, and the exertion of their power forms the muscles, or if the power be not exerted, the muscles, however fully developed previously, must quickly decrease; so it is with the brain, the index of the mind: and as no one can behold the brawny frame of the laborious artisan without being led to consider the exertion of muscular force as the cause of that powerful form, so no one ought to dispute the identical operation in another part of the human system, simply because they *are* familiar with one and *will not* be familiar with the other.

Taking it for granted then, (and surely no one will deny rashly what countless facts have proved, and what is only proved the more as the number of facts increase) that the brain is the organ of the mind, we are led to the following principles.

1. The brain is the organ through which the mind operates.

2. In proportion to the developement of any part of the brain will be the power of that corresponding faculty, sentiment, or passion, because that faculty, sentiment, or passion, by its *anterior action*, has developed the brain.

3. The increase or decrease of mental passions, affections, or sentiments, is accompanied by a corresponding increase or decrease of the brain.

4. The brain like the muscle, is only the agent through which the immaterial spirit acts, for as muscular power resides not in a muscle, so neither does the mind dwell in the brain;—and as all connection between the muscle and life, or vital energy is destroyed by severing the connection of the nerve communicating power to that muscle, so might the mind and brain be severed, but for the beautiful design of Providence, in so carefully protecting the brain lest any mental organ be impaired, as well as by the formation of duplicates to those organs most exposed to injury; for as in common life, the accident that deprives man of a limb, does not render him incapable of his higher and loftier duties, so is it proportionably necessary that the organ through which those higher and nobler functions are performed should have been rendered most secure from harm.

5. That the different parts of the brain having been found by long experience to be appropriated to different functions, those parts are and have the same design, and are produced by the same faculties in all human beings.

Under one of these heads all phrenological facts must fall.

From these principles also, it must be evident that the brain is dependant for its form and character on the developement of the mind in any individual, and in this manner phrenology ascertains the natural bias of the mind, so as to direct education;—it ascertains similarity of pursuits and dispositions so as to improve social intercourse;—it ascertains at any time of life what faculties require to be cultivated or to be checked, what sentiments or passions preponderate in the individual, for good or for evil, what should be repressed, as well as those parts wherein increase should be aimed at, it points out the persons with whom we sympathize, or towards whom we may have an antipathy,—in the treatment of mental disease, its use is obvious. "No more satisfactory proof of this can be referred to, than the extraordinary success of the experiments at the Hanwell Lunatic Asylum under the direction of Dr. and Mrs. Ellis. Regarding the brain not as an entire organized mass, but as an assemblage of organs, some of which may come into a morbid condition while the rest remain comparatively healthy, the course pursued at that excellent institution has been, by kindness and by engaging the attention of the patient, to exercise those organs which are sound, and, by diminishing the action of those which are in a diseased state, to restore them to the healthy performance of their functions. The success which has attended the experiment stands without precedent in the annals of insanity." From this treatment we learn that cures have averaged ninety in a hundred.

Phrenology teaches us how to aim at self-improvement, that is, the duty which every man owes to himself, so as to improve and render more perfect whatsoever is wrong in his nature.—Improvement is the end and object;—it demands a vigorous well regulated exertion of all the energies of thought and feeling.—Phrenology teaches where it is most required—whether it be moral, intellectual or religious, and whichever it may be, we must make it the great end of our endeavours, and use solemnly and deliberately the great powers that GOD has given to us,—without this resolution of purpose the best means are worthless: but with it the poorest may become mighty in moral and intellectual powers, the progression of our nature to the perfection pointed at by St. Paul, must not be regarded as a fiction, but a reality,—we must look coolly and rationally upon the vast amount of ignorance—intemperance, sensuality and selfishness that dwell with and around us,—we must think what an immense field of mind is lost—how many *might be* cheered with intelligence, disinterestedness and refinement, that now *are* lost in voluptuous extravagance or the exercise of worthless and depraved passions;—we must learn the dignity of our station as men—that we shall be made partakers of CHRIST, if we be stedfast unto the end,—and that if we keep this object in view stedfastly and zealously, we shall inherit a crown of righteousness that fadeth not away—and that too in a kingdom of everlasting happiness where the wicked shall cease from troubling and the weary be at rest.

ON THE STRUCTURE AND ANATOMY OF THE BRAIN.

The BRAIN is admitted by physiologists, to be the organ of the mind, although dissection furnishes no clue to its functions, but the same may be said of the eye, the tongue or the ear. The phrenologist compares developement of brain with manifestation of mental power, and by its classification of organs arranges those instruments through which the mind manifests its power during life. A brief description of the brain therefore will be advantageous. It is a mass of soft matter not homogeneous, but presenting different appearances; part of it white in colour, and fibrous in texture is named the *medullary substance* and abounds in the interior; the other matter is of a grey colour and not fibrous in appearance, this forms the outer-portion of brain, they do not blend together, but have a perfect line of distinction. There is no adipose or fatty matter in the skull. The brain is divided into two hemispheres, separated by a strong membrane termed the *Falciform process of the Dura Mater,* and each hemisphere is divided into three lobes, anterior, middle and posterior: the two hemispheres and the organs of each side are brought into communication by fibres running transversely. The *cerebellum and brain* are only slightly and indirectly connected.

The greater portion of the brain is destitute of sensibility, Sir C. Bell imagines from this that it possesses a higher office than that of sensual perception. The external substance of the brain is arranged in convolutions or folds; these appear to be intended for the purpose of increasing its superficial extent with the least enlargement of size,—in the inferior classes of animals there are no convolutions, but they increase in number and extent as we ascend in the scale of being. Each side of the *brain* and also of the *cerebellum,* is supplied with separate arteries conveying blood to it, while the *sinuses* or canals which return the blood to the heart are common to all.

The CEREBELLUM is composed of matter similar to that of the brain in appearance, but different in arrangement,—it is separated from the brain by a strong membrane called the *tentorium*: its fibres originate in the *medulla oblongata* where the organs of the propensities take their rise, so that the *brain and cerebellum* although separated by the *tentorium* are both connected together. The brain and Cerebellum are protected by the skull, and the brain is formed before the bones which invest it. The process of ossification is gradual, the principal portion at birth being strong membranes in which the points of ossification begin and continue increasing in extent and strength till about the age of nine years: between the substance of the brain and the skull are the *pia mater* and the *dura mater,* two integuments which enclose the peripheral extent of the brain and convey blood-vessels to its several parts, the brain with these membranes exactly fills the interior of the skull. The skull fully formed is composed of eight bones which are connected by indented edges: the internal and external surfaces are, from their smooth surface called the *plates* and the intermediate part, *diploe,* which is of a loose cellular texture; as this *diploe* is nearly equally thick in every part, the two tables are nearly parallel to each other, and the variations where they occur do not exceed the eighth or tenth part of an inch; the integuments being an exact form of the brain, and the bony matter fitting them exactly, it follows that there is no obstacle of importance to prevent our observing the form of the brain by the form of the skull.

Disease and old age alone oppose obstacles to this proceeding; for by these causes the skull may be increased or diminished in volume, and it is generally irregular in thickness in old age: the *sutures* also interrupt absolute parallelism, but their situation is known and allowed for, and the *frontal sinus,* or cavity at the top of the nose, in the frontal bone, (which is often enlarged and covered by the *schneiderian membrane* giving great power to the nerves of smell) is so remotely connected that it can only affect a few organs,—five at the most. These few objections are so fully overruled by practice and observation, that they can never lead to error if the student exercise a proper degree of caution.—We may conclude then, that if men manifest their *true nature* in their actions, (and men cannot always be dissemblers,) the mind influencing the brain, and thereby the skull, must present a developement corresponding to their real character—and that PHRENOLOGY or external examination leads to the results sought for when we examine human nature for the purpose of self improvement, or for moral and religious elevation of character.

ON TEMPERAMENT.

The Temperaments are commonly stated to be four only, and their sub-divisions; as these are united in the same individual. These are, the *Nervous, Sanguine, the Bilious, and the Lymphatic*; they are however rarely met with in a separate state, the greater number of persons presenting a mixed temperament, the most predominant of which are the *Sanguine-Bilious* and the *Sanguine-Nervous,* a milder form of *Lymphatic and the Lymphatic* with the *Sanguine, Bilious and Nervous,* may be stated as producing twelve varieties. Temperament may be defined as the natural constitutional tendency of the individual, producing a disposition to exert certain faculties more than others: for this reason they must be carefully studied, that their *active* and *passive* influence upon the mind may be ascertained. Their action is chiefly manifested in the *energy* or *apathy,* of the individual's character; for when properly balanced, by their equal influence on a well cultivated mind, they produce the beautiful harmony of feeling, that leads to a right estimation of things whether moral, intellectual, or physical; by their combined influence in the physical man, that is on the passions and affections, or, on the intellectual being, that is, the perceptives actives, and the reflectives passive,—or upon the higher sentiments, when the moral energy is active, and the spiritual zeal passive,—they produce the noblest developement of character that can actuate human nature—the disunity of these produces but a heathen morality on the one hand, or religious fanaticism on the other: in the mind too, while there is an active *perception* of facts, without due *reflection* on causes, or the reverse of these, the mind may be led into an excess of its favourite pursuit, to the ultimate loss of much mental power. When rightly exercised however, the spiritual unity of body, mind and soul, produces a vigorous pursuit of whatever is great and good in human nature.

The Temperaments may be generally referred to some particular constitution of the organic system—whole families are sometimes of a similar temperament, and at others no two members are alike: a great portion probably depends upon parental causes, in the same way that family likenesses are often observed, probably they may be referred to the blood as a chief cause, the active circulation producing great action on the brain and nerves originating the *nervous*: a fulness of the circulating medium may produce the *sanguine*; a muscular developement the *bilious*; a sluggish system the *lymphatic*. The classification of the temperaments, and their combined influence upon the three-fold nature of man may be best understood from careful observation: when pure they present the following appearances;—

1. A NERVOUS TEMPERAMENT is indicated by a pale complexion, features sharp and angular, delicate texture of the muscular system, fine silky hair, delicate

health, quickness of perception and great susceptibility; persons under the influence of this temperament are very sensitive,—act more from impulse and feeling than from principle, and feel great languor when exhausted.

2. The LYMPHATIC TEMPERAMENT, is marked by a full fleshy outline,—round features,—pale complexion, light straightish hair,—pulse slow, muscles soft and the disposition lukewarm and indolent: the circulation being feeble, the mental manifestations are proportionately sluggish and weak.

3. The BILIOUS TEMPERAMENT is distinguished by dark hair, skin of a yellow hue and coarse angular features, eyes active, and often with a severe expression, the muscles firm and well developed;—the pulsations partake of great energy which extends also to the brain.

4. The SANGUINE TEMPERAMENT is evident from a clear florid complexion,—features well formed and fleshy,—the muscles full and tolerably firm, mild expression in the eye,—auburn or brown hair, eyes blue or sometimes hazel,—disposition lively and cheerful.

These, with their combinations will produce all the common varieties, and where they are well united in a single individual the union generally improves the character.

ON THE VARIETIES OF THE HUMAN RACE.

When we regard the different quarters of the globe,—the distinct and permanent features of national character that stamp races of men as races, we are immediately struck with the great mental and natural dissimilarity of these varieties of the human race.—The Briton bowing in worship to the one true and ever living God,—the wild Indian revelling in the uncontrolled sublimities of a wild and unconquered waste,—the Brahmin, prostrate at the blood stained relics of human sacrifice, or the ignorant African, worshipping the carved effigy of some mis-shapen and hideous monster;—each present characters which indicate some strongly marked feature of individual and national constitution. The millions that dwell around the Ganges have a national and characteristic feature in their mental constitution, and this distinguishing mark is as decidedly evident in the form of the brain as it is in the customs of the people,—the same remark applies to all other races;—the European who has long dwelt in a high state of civilization, and mental culture,—The Asiatic, whose ancient customs, moderns vainly seek to improve,—The American, in his native forest, surrounded by civilization, remains even yet in the state of rude and ancient barbarism.—These differences of *national* character, must have a great influence upon the *individual*: the unvarying customs produce a sameness in the organization—the people as a *whole* are intellectual, ignorant, or barbarian.

These national differences have been attributed to the influence of soil and climate:—but although these exercise some influence, they are inadequate to explain the whole—climate would materially affect the customs of the people, and these customs would influence the organization of those parts of the brain influenced by the operations of the mind in procuring animal comforts,—the developement of constructiveness is greatly affected by the cause. But when we remember how certainly the same causes produce the same results throughout the works of nature, we are often unable to explain much of this influence, the Europeans and native Indians have lived for centuries under the influence of the same physical causes—the one has progressed like their brethren of the old continent,—the other remains stationary in savage and uncivilized wildness.

Religious and political institutions again, have been brought forward as the causes of these differences; but this is a superficial view of the matter, because it will be granted that all our institutions have been framed as the minds of man require them, not anteriorly: and when we except institutions like that of christianity, the direct gift of God himself, from what cause do we consider human institutions to emanate except from the minds of those who legislate for the wants of a people, or who impose institutions upon them by right of arbitrary power.

That national character accords with Phrenological rules, is true as far as we have opportunities of judging; but at present our collections of national skulls are not sufficiently extensive to draw any very remarkable conclusions; the most prejudiced observer cannot fail to remark the great difference among the skulls of different people—thus, the ancient Greek with *Ideality and Constructiveness* large, when opposed to the deficient skull of the New Hollander, shews as striking a contrast, as the hovels of the one, do to the architectural remains of the other.[1]

To estimate national peculiarities properly, travellers competent to examine heads, and classify temperaments are much wanted: the size of individual organs and their combinations are also required: the skulls that we possess shew that the brain is in exact agreement with the characters given to their various people by travellers of observation and experience.—The subjugation of a free people to a foreign yoke,—the introduction of new customs by conquerors,—the revolutions of states and empires, and the intercourse of nations, with many other matters to be gathered from the history of the world, all aid in assisting us to determine national character and from this to deduce the natural tendencies of individuals.

[1] No one will doubt how much influence Christianity has had in producing the high moral and intellectual developement of Europeans, to this also we may trace their great intellectual superiority as nations.

MENTAL FACULTIES.

DIVISION I.
FEELINGS AND PROPENSITIES.

Common to man and the inferior animals.

1. Amativeness. Love.

This organ is situated in the cerebellum, about half way between the centre of the occipital bone and the large long process behind the ear. It manifests itself by the thickness or width of the back part of the head; it is produced as the human frame approaches full developement, being small in children, and generally on the increase between the ages of sixteen and twenty four,—it frequently diminishes in old age. USE,—This organ is properly exercised in virtuous affection:—the endearments of a domestic circle, and the society of those we love;—it softens the proud, irascible, anti-social principles of human nature, and aids the benevolent affections,—it causes a respectful, and honourable deference to the softer sex;—inspires the poet in his best conceptions of the purity, and self devotedness of Love, and produces that quiet but effectual influence in society, which is shown in the kind interest taken by either sex in the proceedings of the other. When abused, or allowed only to act as an animal propensity, the absence of the higher feature is a very unamiable trait in the human character,—no deference is paid to age or sex and woman regarded only as the minister to illicit lust. Love to God is shown by overcoming these baser feelings, "they who love me, are such as follow my commands" were the words of the Christian's pattern, and the exercise of this mental faculty is best shown by those who practise charity or universal love without which we are but as "a sounding brass or tinkling cymbal." ABUSE.—An encouragement of animal and debasing sensuality which soon leads to a loss of modesty, and personal respect, and virtue: the worship due to the Creator is lavished on the creature; Jealousy and its myriad evil attendants originate chiefly in the abuse of this faculty.

2. Philoprogenitiveness, Love of Offspring.

In animals this organ is termed *instinct*, and instinct means an original propensity impelling an animal to a particular action without intention or purpose. This organ is situated over the cerebellum, and corresponds to the protuberance of the occiput, rather above and between the duplex organ of amativeness. As a faculty inherent in the human race it is beautifully shown in parental affection; women have it larger than men, and it is found to be larger in the female, than in the male skulls of animals. The interest of this feeling is often proportionate to the helplessness of infancy;—a mother doats on her infant in the earliest months of existence when few beside herself can see any attractions in it: it is generally manifested in large families where the youngest is invariably the favourite, unless when sickness causes another to share in maternal tenderness. It seems probable that the fondness lavished by maiden ladies on animals, originates in this faculty: for they often nurse and pamper their pets quite as excessively as parents do children. The mutual love or affection for the same offspring is the bond of union in marriage—a step-parent seldom exhibits any thing more than regard towards the child of another: it has been observed by Spurzheim that he found it small in 29 infanticides whom he had been able to examine: but as the faculty in its proper use produces feelings of the most delightful and exquisite character so is it the more liable to ABUSE. Children are thus spoiled by indulgence, their prospects are raised by a parent's mistaken affection; and instead of protection and happiness to children and attention and deference from them, it too often terminates in a spoiled child on the one side, and disrespect towards the other. Through mistaken opinions parents often prefer to make their children *rich* rather than *good* thus sacrificing their temporal and eternal welfare, leading them to put their trust in things "which the moth and rust doth corrupt and where thieves do break in and steal," rather than in that Rock of ages without whose knowledge not one sparrow dies.

3. Adhesiveness, Attachment.

This organ is located at the middle of the posterior edge of the parietal lobe, or each side of Concentrativeness, higher than Philoprogenitiveness, and just above the lambdoidal suture. USE—This faculty is marked in those individuals who exhibit permanent attachment to beings and objects around them—it gives a permanence to friendship, a steady adherence to opinions, and a dislike to change whether of objects or persons: a person with this faculty well developed will manifest friendship to another even in the greatest depression of fortune when friendship is most severely tried: it is on the average larger in females than in men, and this is shewn in the permanence of their attachments, "Man," it is said "may love, but it is too often with a view to his own gratification, but when a woman loves, she does so with all her soul."—The absence of this organ shews an individual to be of a cold, indifferent character in his friendship, and one not to be depended upon in the hour of misfortune, it is only where the organ is well developed that an attachment is sustained through evil report and good report: when regulated by judgment rather than passion, it produces the noblest examples of disinterestedness and devotion.—The ABUSE of this organ is shown in the unworthy attachment of man to the fleeting things of this life—he places not his affections upon high, but on the conections of party, the interests, the advantages of this life—he loves life to an erroneous extent, perhaps degenerates into a recluse, shews a devoted attachment to the good things of this life and but little for him who was the true friend as "the way, the truth, and the life."

4. Inhabitiveness.—Love of Home.

Inhabitiveness is by many persons considered as a modification of the preceding organ or of *Concentrativeness*: it can hardly be considered a definite organ, or a distinct mental faculty: it is observed particularly in the attachment of individuals to some particular spot,—their home, country, or abode of those whom they love;—as the Swiss have been known to pine for the mountain heights of their father land, or, as all men desire their ashes to repose at the side of their dearest kin. Dr. Spurzheim in his late work published in America is inclined to attribute a more extensive sphere of action to this organ than can be yet decided; and in fact, it is a decided manifestation of mental energy in many persons—a dislike of change, especially of abode; a disinclination to travel, an attachment to the place of birth, of long residence, or the spot where life has been spent, leads many persons to live and die in the same spot where their fathers lived and died before them;—it is this organ that gives a *Home* to Englishmen, *Home,* for which some languages have not even an expression, *Home,* in defence of which, Englishmen have so bravely fought, so nobly died. Many animals are attached to peculiar situations, the chamois, on the Alpine cliff,—the eagle, soaring to his eyrie,—and the beaver located by some unfrequented stream, give evidence of a similar tendency.

The faculty when ABUSED, or allowed to be excessive leads to peculiarity of disposition, an avoidance of strangers, a dislike to necessary duties that interfere with domestic arrangements, nervous ideas, susceptibility of insult, and in some cases, by the neglect of external objects, the mind dwelling upon its own internal emotions only, has declined to monomania or even temporary alienation.

5. Combativeness.

Combativeness is situated on each side of Philoprogenitiveness, a little behind, and up from the ear; being the result of great mental energy, it is indicative of physical courage; it enables an individual to contend with difficulty and danger, prompts to repel whatever is inimical, and opposed to his exertions. The instinctive tendency is doubtless to oppose, and thus produce courage; in its lowest activity it leads simply to resistance; in a higher degree to attack the measures, sentiments, or opinions of others; it is generally more developed in men than in women, although individual instances occur among women with this organ largely developed: the name given to this faculty originally by Dr. Gall was, "*the instinct of self defence, and defence of property,*" but the definition was regarded by Spurzheim as too limited; and its operation in connection with other faculties is very extensive indeed—because *courage* when properly directed is useful to preserve the right, and Dr. Johnson speaking of courage, says, "it is a quality so necessary for maintaining virtue that it is respected even when associated with vice."—On this account it lends *energy of character,* and is necessary to all great actions; for even in the most virtuous designs, how frequently is opposition manifested, which it requires every energy to subdue; those who fight for virtue, require courage as much, or more than those who fight for vice;—when this organ is deficient, the individual is unfitted for the bustles and fatigues of active life, he shrinks from hostility and from any course that opposes the feelings, the prejudices or even the vices of human society. It is very powerful in combination, lending its aid to the designs of a Howard, lending *energy* to the application of talent, or *courage* to the opponent of sin;—the most perfect and useful member of society, is formed by the full developement of moral sentiments, due allowance of reflective power, and a stimulative degree of this organ. Useful, however as it is, when well used, so is its action dangerous when unchecked, and in abuse. It inspires a love of contention, and controversy, so that the social hours become embittered by strife; a tendency to anger and provocation by irritating conduct; to rashness in designs from miscalculation of their effects. An individual knowing this organ to be large, should always *think* before he *acts*, and always keep before him the illustrious example of *Him,* who "being reviled, reviled not again."—The energy given him, should be employed well, he should never "be weary of well doing," but remember that "the fruit of the spirit, is love, joy, and peace."

6. Destructiveness.

The organ of destructiveness is immediately over the external opening of the ear, being more or less forward as the developement is more or less intellectual. The faculty is indispensable to all animals who live on flesh, and it differs from the preceding organ in being more permanent. Combativeness gives courage to meet danger, or oppose it without terror. Destructiveness lends a *constant power* of overcoming and destroying as long as the object of opposition remains; its energy is thus a permanent stimulus to exertion, so as to overcome whatever object is in view—if learning, indefatigable perseverance; if riches, a constant plodding in the pursuit; if virtue, a firm and unvarying opposition to the myriad phases of sin. Combativeness is the *active* momentary stimulus that requires excitement. Destructiveness, the *passive* energy that supports continued exertion. The organ is thus valuable when rightly used, but unfortunately it lends its energy to evil pursuits as well as good ones—it is found in the hardened and unrepentant sinner, as well as in the noble and energetic patriot; it is thus highly dangerous in persons whose organization is not under the government of moral principle; a good endowment is indispensable for a proper discharge of duty, as the sword, the emblem of destructiveness is often combined with the scales of justice, the one to measure the offence, the other to punish the contemners of the law; those who have the organ small, are deficient of energy, incapable of fighting with the turmoils of the world.—on the other hand the abuse of it is recognised in petty tyranny, a desire to trample on those beneath us; a carelessness to the happiness of others, and a severity of punishment for the minutest fault; In common life we may trace the operation of this faculty; a preacher, with the organ large and benevolence small, would hold out the *threatenings* of the Gospel, a preacher of the opposite organization would dwell upon its *promise of pardon*; the ill-treatment of animals and children, results from this faculty, uncontrolled by moral sentiments; the crowds of ignorant persons who assemble at bull-baits, cock fights, and other species of cruelty are led to gratify the organ from a want of moral principle: the dreadful practice of swearing, uttering threats of vengeance far beyond human power, and calling down imprecations on the heads of others, arises from the same cause, and how rarely are these seen (to any extent) in educated society—where the energy of character has been directed by moral training into useful channels;—The abuse of this organ is therefore to be earnestly cautioned against, because, lending its energy to evil, it is productive of the worst results. Destructiveness itself is rarely found as a principle of destruction, but the various degrees of vice and crime are often persevered in till they become more evil than this organ. A person therefore should endeavour to break off rooted habits (if bad ones) by directing the energy of the mind into other channels, they must walk in the Spirit, and not fulfil the lusts of the flesh, knowing that, "they that are Christ's crucify the flesh and the affections, and lusts that belong to it." Let them put on the whole armour of God, so that they may stand against the wiles of the devil, let them take the helmet of salvation and the sword of the spirit, which is the WORD OF GOD.

7. Secretiveness.

This organ is situated immediately above Destructiveness, in the lateral portion of the brain; when both organs are fully developed, it becomes difficult without practice to distinguish them, it may therefore be mentioned that Secretiveness is higher and more forward than the other. It seems to result from some instinctive tendency existing in the mind, to conceal from the public eye, its own emotions and ideas. It is essential to a prudent character, for as Solomon says, "A fool uttereth all his mind; but a wise man keepeth it in till afterwards."—In the lower order of animals the same faculty is termed *cunning*, and it not only aids them in their pursuit of food, but also enables them to combat force by prudence. It enforces a salutary restraint against undue manifestation of other propensities which are best maintained within an individual's own bosom, and it serves likewise to guard against the prying curiosity of others; those persons in whom it is deficient are blunt and unrestrained in their opinions, exhibit great want of tact in society, expressing their sentiments without regard to propriety of time, or place, or person. When properly employed, this organ tends to shew a reserved disposition, it suspects the secret design of others, and exhibits the secrecy which is indispensable to prudent conduct and success: a deficiency of this organ is shown among tale bearers, gossips, and newsmongers, and to the want of it some portion of scandal may be attributed. Secretiveness is necessary for the confidence of friendship, it is an essential element of politeness, much of which consists in avoiding the expression of what is disagreeable. It is however liable to ABUSE, and then it leads to much evil: a love for concealment, intrigue, cunning, and mystery in the details of every day life; hypocrisy and dissimulation to hide what has been done on the sly; persons with overweening *Self Esteem* always conceal their affairs from the eye of the world, are anxious to support appearances, and maintain a fair character outwardly even if their private acts are of the grossest kind; if associated with want of moral sentiment it leads to lying and theft: it is often manifest to a surprising extent among the insane. Persons having the organ large will do well to keep a check upon any unnatural reserve: and they should always see that they do nothing that requires concealment: if the organ *must be* exercised, let them lay up the word of God in their hearts which is the seed, that sown in an honest and good heart, brings forth fruit to perfection.

8. Alimentiveness.

This organ is only a probable one: a love for food hardly appears to be a natural function of the mind, and most of the known instances of enormous appetite appear to have resulted from organic disease (in nearly every instance that is quoted by Phrenologists.) There appears to be some grounds for supposing that this part of the brain is connected with the sensations of hunger and thirst, and perhaps also with the sense of taste. Spurzheim says of it, "This organ though indicated by reason and comparative anatomy, is merely probable and can be confirmed or rejected like every other, according to direct observations alone, in comparing cerebral developement to the special propensity. I possess many facts in confirmation."

9. Constructiveness, Mechanical Skill.

It requires some little experience to tell the precise spot of this organ, it is situated in the frontal bone above the spheno-temporal suture, but its position varies with the developement; and it is somewhat covered by the temporal muscle, so that it is difficult to judge except from experience. Constructiveness is the application of the inventive faculty, and since necessity is the mother of invention, Constructiveness is that talent possessed by man for constructing and fabricating whatever his wants or his desires may originate. It is this organ that is exercised by the architect, the painter and the poet in refined life, by the artisan of humble life, by the beaver in their huts, birds in their nests and even spiders in their webs: it is a most valuable faculty: and to it we are indebted for the ability to carry out what the mere intellectual faculties have conceived: it depends for its value upon the organs wherewith it is associated, with language and Ideality, it gives poetical ability; with form, the art of sculpture; or with colour, painting—where the organ is in excess it determines to ABUSE; such as, the attempting to do what an acquaintance with philosophy would prove impossible; the construction of ingenious, but useless or even mischievous articles; the application of constructive ability in imitating valuables for base purposes; throwing away great labour on articles of curiosity, and innumerable other ways in which mis-application of ability is productive of injury: it should be remembered that ability in any way is a talent, for us to improve against the time when our Lord comes to require it of us, and we should remember that misapplication will be a more serious fault, than that of the servant who hid his lord's talent in a napkin, or of him who buried it in the ground.

10. Acquisitiveness.

This organ is situated at the inferior range of the parietal bone. The faculty of the mind is a tendency to *acquire* whatever is regarded valuable and whether riches or learning or articles of vertu be the object of acquisition, there appears to be little doubt, that such a faculty is natural to the nature of man. Although such an instinctive desire presents the aspect of meanness we must in some measure look at its effects; what would England or any civilized country be, if there had never been a desire for storing up the products of intellect and philosophy,—and the wealth that enables England to send out millions in spreading the word of God over a benighted and barbarous world?—If industry were to be limited by present wants, man would always continue the creature of mere impulse; it is the faculty of acquisitiveness that directs a systematic aim at supplying the comforts and elegancies of life, and to this, accumulation is necessary: when however the pursuit of wealth becomes the chief business of life the moral sentiments are deadened, the intellect and the nobler faculties of the mind become engrossed in a debasing pursuit, the sympathy that characterizes a true christian is lost sight of. To provide for immediate wants of ourselves and those dependant upon us, to furnish the means of some repose for the body so as to enable the mind to enjoy cultivation, and to provide for the education of offspring:—to give a natural tendency for learning, for religious instruction, or the acquisition of that knowledge which is power, may be set down as the proper objects of this faculty: where the faculty of acquisitiveness is unduly exercised, and the propensity to acquire is not balanced by veneration and conscientiousness, the character is often influenced to dishonesty. In ABUSE; a miserly hoarding and total neglect of charity is evident, covetousness which St Paul condemns as idolatry, avarice and selfishness, a total disregard of distress, of conscientious principle, and of honour and duty are first and foremost;—from this organ, the weak fall a prey to the strong, the poor to the avarice of the lovers of mammon as they are called, that riches are valued more than public virtue or private integrity—that riches are pursued to the total ruin of the loftier principles of human nature, and to this prostitution of spirit and of soul is owing the difficulty of a rich man's entering the kingdom of heaven. If there be such an instinctive tendency of the human mind, no better advice can ever be offered than that of the christian's pattern "seek ye first the kingdom of God and his righteousness and all other things shall be added unto you." "For what shall it profit a man, if he gain the whole world, and lose his own soul?"—

Besides these organs of the propensities, phrenologists have imagined the existence of a peculiar instinct termed *Vitativeness*, or love of life: the fact is probable but requires much caution and much experience before it can be definitely decided: the existence of a few isolated facts does not necessarily include the whole human race as being like a few individuals, and there is great necessity for not increasing the number of organs without due confirmation, because the simplicity of arrangement and the plainness of the science is thereby disturbed. Of this organ Spurzheim says "I look for this organ at the basis, where the middle and posterior lobes of the brain meet each other, at the internal border of Combativeness."

DIVISION II.
INTELLECTUAL AND PERCEPTIVE FACULTIES OF THE MIND.

11. Language.

It was owing to this organ, a full prominent eye, that Dr Gall first directed his attention to a scientific investigation of the faculties of the mind. vide Page. 5

A large developement is indicated by the prominence and depression of the eye, this appearance being produced by convolutions of the brain situated in the posterior and transverse part of the orbitary plate, pressing downward and outward in proportion to its convolutions. A full developement of this organ indicates a faculty for the acquisition and employment of words, or artificial signs, expressing our ideas; the meaning of the signs must be determined by other faculties, exactly as force or power of any kind requires to be guided and directed: from this reason may originate the very different significations given to the same abstract word, a different organization producing a difference in the meaning attached to it in spite of every effort to give an accurate definition; this will be self evident, if we merely quote the three leading features of Christianity, Faith, Hope, and Charity, and refer to different degrees of moral and intellectual elevation or turpitude, for the vague, unsatisfactory, and degraded meaning that we find frequently attached to them. Persons with a large endowment of this faculty, abound in words; in conversation they pour forth with volubility, but when excited they pour forth a torrent; this should be moderated by good sense, and appropriate language rather than verbosity will be employed in their speaking efforts as well as in their writings: when the organ is deficient, the individual wants a command of expression, he writes and speaks with great poverty of style, and when possessed of ideas is unable to clothe them in elegant or even appropriate language. The talent for, or facility of learning foreign languages originates in the same faculty, taken connectedly with the mental capacity for entering into the style and combinations of other countries. Some individuals in whom the organ is large do not necessarily possess a ready memory, which usually occurs when the faculty that apprehends the primitive idea (of which words only pronounce the name) is more than ordinarily small. The organ abused generally makes a speechifier of small worth, a talker for the mere sake of talking, who frequently loses sight of reason and subject as well as his own good sense.—Its best use is a felicity of diction in describing the sentiments and opinions of the individual so that they may be exactly comprehended by others.

12. Form.

This organ is situated in the corner of the eye next the nose, and when large there is a considerable breadth across the nose at that place: its chief use is in the accurate knowledge of form, whether of persons or objects, and disposes the mind to give a definite form to objects even when unseen: it is to this the acute observation of objects, by which means we compare them one with another, or personal identity after absence and probable change in the form of features: to this organ many distinguished sculptors and architects owe much of their excellence, as its necessary action in connection with other organs would be to express an accuracy of outline: it is to an excessive use of this organ that painters study correctness of form in drawing, and neglect colouring; useful to architects for this reason.

13. Size.

The organ of size is situated at the corner of the eyebrow, next to individuality, and appears to influence the capability of the eye and mind in its motions of dimension: instances are known where persons deficient in this faculty have been unable to manage perspective in drawings, or even to copy the plainest figure without error in the size: others on the contrary measure size by the eye almost as accurately as by a rule, and are especially accurate in judging about dimensions—the organ is necessary for some professions, but not of great general importance.

14. Weight.

This faculty like the preceding, is shewn only in particular persons: the absence of it is rarely noticed, and the presence of it quite unseen except in some particular walks of life. It gives a power of measuring, and comprehending the resistance of bodies to forces applied to them, is useful in philosophic enquiry, engineering, architecture &c.

15. Colouring.

The sensation of colour on the eye is very different in different persons; many persons having an acute sense of vision readily perceive the qualities of objects but are incapable of judging about the agreement or disagreement of particular colours, and when the faculty is small they confound them and are incapable of perceiving their effect. When prominent the individual possesses a taste for gaudy colours, careless about their arrangement or harmony with others. It is situated in the centre of the eyebrow giving it a prominent aspect such as may be witnessed in the portraits of Titian, Rubens, and many celebrated artists: The organ of colour well developed gives harmony and excellence in colouring and is useful to botanists, dyers, mercers, and all artists: That the faculty is abused, or rather wanting may be witnessed by the numberless facts that we meet with constantly, where people dress in gaudy colours and appear quite regardless of their being suitable or otherwise.

16. Space.

This hardly appears a positive faculty, we have noticed it from its being mentioned by phrenologists; it appears to be of a similar kind to form, size, and weight, all of which organs are connected with the organ of vision; the persons who have the organ well developed are persons of wide views in every thing, they are enraptured with extensive prospects, mountains, and every thing of a large size—if proved to exist, such a faculty would be valuable to painters.

17. Order.

The tendency of this faculty is to produce a love of order and arrangement in every thing; they are distressed by confusion, and are highly pleased with a regular arrangement of their furniture, books and other property. The organ is located in the superciliary ridge, and from its general small developement, much fact is still necessary before the organ and its value can be definitely determined: there is certainly well marked in some persons, a love of order, and in others a carelessness to disorder, the one often degenerating into precision in trifles that produces great discomfort to other persons, the latter often inducing a disregard of necessary care and attention: the medium is to be sought for by all who detect either in their own character.

18. Number.

The organ of the faculty of NUMBER is situated above and outside the external angle of the eye, a little below the external angle of the frontal bone. The special function seems to be calculation in general: it does not seem to extend to any faculty of computation beyond that of numbers, although from the tact that it associates with it, it facilitates the study of mathematics. Many instances are adduced of its large size in good calculators, particularly in George Bidder, the calculating boy. This organ, like the other perceptives requires cultivation.

19. Tune.

The organ of TUNE bears the same relation to the ears that the organ of *Colouring* does to the eyes. A large developement of the organ enlarges the lateral parts of the forehead, and great practice is always necessary before the organ can be successfully observed: but if two persons are placed together, the one having it largely, the other smally developed, the superior one will be perceptible at a glance. The faculty gives the perception of melody, which is only *one* of the ingredients of musical talent; the organs of the mind must be well developed in accordance with this, so that the soul and expression of music may be felt and appreciated, before the organs are perfectly developed; the fingers indeed may be trained to great expertness, but it is only the real lover of harmonious sounds who devotes *all* his powers to its cultivation that can arrive at any thing like perfect skill. As a natural faculty of nature, this organ is particularly pleasing in calming the passions, and producing pleasure by means perfectly innocent. Persons cannot obtain a scientific knowledge of music in whom the organ is deficient, and when *abused* as this faculty often is, it should be remembered that the line between pleasure and pain is so indefinite, that where one terminates the other begins;—music carried beyond an agreeable pitch, leads the possessor into society, and too frequently into pleasures more enervating and sensual—these are to be dreaded, and the musician should remember that as the noblest employment of his faculty is to "Praise God in the highest,"—so, nothing can be more debasing than the prostitution of it to unworthy purposes.

20. Time.

The organ of Time seems to be related to that of order in its effects, it is essential to music and versification, form some source of pleasure in dancing, and seems to give a power of judging time and intervals of duration in general. The value of time renders this faculty more than usually necessary; it leads to a right estimation of punctuality as well as punctuality in engagements. persons with the organ large are fevered by delay, they become irritated about trifles of time that they may be kept waiting by others and thus incur a charge of bad temper. The organ is especially useful in persons studying history as it tends to give a faculty of remembering dates and other periods of time, the succession of events, &c.

21. Locality.

Dr. Gall was led to infer the position of this organ from witnessing the memory of particular persons in their relation of places they had visited, and the strong impression made upon them by surrounding objects, so that he regarded this to be a primitive faculty. Spurzheim says, "the special faculty of this organ and the sphere of its activity, remains to be determined. It makes the traveller, geographer and landscape painter, recollects localities and gives notions of perspective." Persons in whom the organ is large, form vivid and distinct conceptions of situations and scenery which they have seen or heard described, and have great power in recalling such conceptions.—The organ is large in all eminent navigators and travellers, also in great astronomers and geographers. Persons who have this organ large, are passionately fond of travelling: and where firmness is small, it influences to restlessness, and love of change; to physical pleasure as a gratification of this organ, in the neglect of other duties, and thus often exerts a baneful influence on the mind when allowed to operate without control.

22. Individuality.

The tendency of this organ is, the examination of fact as the only foundation of truth; it is situated in the middle of the lower part of the forehead, immediately above the top of the nose, it produces breadth and projection between the eyebrows. This faculty renders us observant of outward objects, and gives a desire to know, and to examine; it prompts to observation and general information, and is necessary for the acquisition of facts as a basis of science. Spurzheim says, "Persons endowed with this faculty in a high degree are attentive to all that happens around them, to every object, to every phenomenon, to every fact: it desires to know all by experience, and consequently puts every other organ into action: is fond of instruction, collects facts, and leads to practical knowledge."—To the influence of this organ we may trace the knowledge of individuals by animals, and even wild beasts in which this organ is large may be tamed to the will of a keeper. It puts into active exertion the perceptive faculties round the eyebrow, and thus influences the quality of the faculty (language) which lies in that portion of brain; so that a person with this organ large, and language small, will say but a few words and those to the purpose, or with individuality small and language large, he will utter ten thousand neatly turned sentences of the meanest commonplace, alike destitute of information or science. Persons in whom the organ is large, are alive to every thing that passes around them, they look at facts and events, leaving it to others to reason upon them, and many great discoveries have been made by persons with this organ large who have not been celebrated for their powers of reasoning. When the organ is small, the individual fails to observe things that are going on around him, he will walk in the streets, or the country and see or rather observe literally nothing; he may visit a house without observing any one object beyond the immediate purpose of his visit.

Abuses. This organ is often employed in the affairs of other people, in petty knowledge that tends to no real purpose; a superficiality of observation that leads to erroneous inferences, and when largely developed with the reflective and philosophic faculties, it leads to peculiarity of studies and pursuits to the exclusion of all others, and by breaking the unity of learning which points all things to Him who gave, it is too often the cause, of mistaken opinion or downright error.

23. Eventuality.

Enquires into events and takes notice of occurrences; it gives prominence, or a rounded fulness to the middle of the forehead. Dr. Gall comprised this organ and the preceding one in one faculty, but it is now known that the one takes cognizance of objects, the other the relationship and actions of those objects. It seems to unite the reflectives with the perceptives, so that it recognizes the activity of other faculties and directs them to strict action; it desires to know by experience, and thus produces what is termed the *good sense* of a matter, and by recognizing the functions of the other powers of the brain and the operations of the external senses, it reduces those impressions into conceptions, ideas and opinions.—Eventuality is shewn when we review the past for comparison with the future, it examines the effects of God's government in the universe and brings home the truths of the gospel to the heart of every one. Eventuality is the intellectual door to the threefold nature of man directing facts to his perceptive, reflective and moral being, thus pointing out the truth of Christianity in the fulfilment of prophecy, the mercy of the Creator and the punishment entailed upon sin; without this faculty the mind acquires a false conception of things, unsound opinions, and a tendency to the doctrines of materialism and infidelity from the animal rather than the intellectual nature being appealed to. Persons distinguished in professional pursuits have this organ large, since they possess readiness of observation as well as talent in the detail, whereby previously acquired knowledge is brought to bear upon present emergencies; where the organ is only partially and imperfectly developed, he will feel great difficulty in commanding his knowledge or appealing to it with any certainty, the organ should therefore be assiduously cultivated. In ABUSE it tends to promote a love of trifles, detailed events, scandal and abuse, the minutest particulars in preference to general information and individual aggrandizement rather than general good.

24. Comparison.

The organ of comparison lies upon the upper and middle portion of the frontal bone. The aim of the faculty seems to be to form abstract ideas, generalizations and establish harmony among the operations of the other faculties; thus comparing and establishing analogies among the objects of which a knowledge has been obtained by the perceptives: and it not only traces real resemblances, but the relations which things have to one another; persons with this organ large illustrate their ideas by similies drawn from other objects and thus render them plainer to the understanding of another person, and the comparisons thus drawn will be derived from those objects which most commonly engage the attention of the person making them: it is generally large in poets, even when they write prose; 2,500 similies are found in *Moore's Life of Sheridan*; these comparisons please, because they address themselves to the multitude and produce clearness and force of illustration. Spurzheim says of this organ, "In order to persuade and to affect, the speaker or orator must speak by analogy, he must bring spiritual things close to terrestrial objects and compare them with each other; the activity of this faculty is very important, it compares the sensations and ideas of all the other faculties and points out their difference, analogy, similitude, or identity." By comparison, man is enabled to judge whether his own life is *what it ought to be*, whether he has lived for *time* or for *eternity*: by comparison he is enabled to determine how far his life agrees with the Christian's pattern, knowing that "as he sows, so will he reap;" the propensities incline to evil, as a necessary sequence to the fall, the moral sentiments urge on to good, a foreshadowing of immortality, the reflectives teach him *how* to be good, how to compare the truth as it is in Christ Jesus, with his own sinful heart, and learn wherein he errs. This is the proper and should be the only true aim of the Christian. In ABUSE this faculty frequently leads to false reasoning on account of the inactivity of the perceptives, in examining the subjects compared, it gives a love for similies and analogies, not always caring for their applicability, and unless duly regulated by the nobler instincts of fallen humanity, it degenerates to sophistry and a blindness to error.

25. Causality.

This organ lies immediately at the sides of *Comparison* and is found large in men distinguished for profound metaphysical talent. We have shown how *Individuality* and *Eventuality* take cognizance of things evident to the senses; Causality looks to the *cause* of the phenomena observed by other faculties: it expresses the irresistible conviction that every phenomenon and change around us emanates from a mighty, an unseen, an Eternal God; it looks to Him as the cause of our joys, and our possessions here, as the omniscient and ever merciful Father who gave his Son to die for our transgressions, it seeks Him as the cause of our hopes of everlasting bliss, and it bids us to acknowledge and adore. It is the faculty that considers the relation of cause and effect and prompts the question, *Why?* to whatever is unknown, or imperfectly understood; and for this reason requires to be watched lest the matter of enquiry be placed beyond the limited faculties of man, and infinite subjects be thus reasoned upon by finite capacity. If this organ be in unity with *Veneration, Conscientiousness*, and *Comparison*, the individual will be of steady, and rational Christian principles, but if without them, impious doubts and atheistical surmises will tend to require a *visible* cause for what must be *invisible* and the germ of error being planted, it may take root and abound to the ruin of nobler and more elevating opinions. In ABUSE, this organ produces a mania for possibilities, denying the existence of causes not evident to the senses, a disbelief in whatever is spiritual, and a direct influence to intellectual pride, sophistry, and error.

26. Gaiety.

The organ of Gaiety is sometimes called Wit; and has been defined by Spurzheim as "a sentiment which disposes men to view every thing in a gay, joyful, and mirthful manner;"—"given to man to render him merry and gay,—feelings not to be confounded with satisfaction and contentment." The faculty appears to give a characteristic tendency to view every thing that occurs in a light manner, simply as far as it gratifies, and pleases, not in proportion to its intrinsic value, combined with the higher faculties, it produces wit, in common events humour; with the animal propensities, sarcasm and satire, or caricature and excess; with language, punning and double meanings, and in all cases it tends to a levity that is often misplaced. It is situated between Ideality and Causality at the upper part of the side of the forehead. In ABUSE, or when not counteracted by reason and reflection, it tends to severity and satirical remarks on the failings and weaknesses of others: a too easy regard for sin when not positively offensive, a love of pleasure, often leading to vicious excess; and frequently the faculty to gratify itself, offends friends by ill timed remarks and a system of practical jokes.

This organ acting upon the intellect leads to unsound and hasty judgments, because the mind being influenced more by *Ideality* than *Causality*, (between which two organs *Gaiety* is situated) it becomes an enemy to self discipline, and study, and leads the possesser into a physical love of pleasure, &c.—it opposes also the operation of the higher intellectual faculties from its close approximation to the true organ of analogy which is situated between the duplex organ of *Causality* in the centre of the forehead, and by a vain influence on the imagination it leads to delusive analogies as regards truth, overcoming the careful study of fact by the perceptive faculties and diverting the current of conscious inquiry by a regard for self and its pleasures rather than the true and correct analogies of truth.

27. Imitation.

Imitation leads us to imitate what we see deserving to be copied in others, and thus lies at the foundation of all art, because it is necessary to copy before any skill can be arrived at. It is a necessary ingredient in the character of actors, sculptors, architects, painters and engravers: it influences the style of the author, the manner of the poet, the correctness of the dramatist. It is always active in children and thus forms a natural education in them, taken from the persons around them: it is for this reason essentially and imperatively necessary that good models are presented to children in their youth; it gives a talent of acquiring the peculiarity of foreign languages; and when deficient, it produces a stiffness and uncomfortable mannerism that causes a person to appear like a fish out of water. It may be misused by being employed for mimicry and buffoonery especially for defects—in vice this is the real "facilis descensus averni,"—The situation of the faculty on either side of Benevolence, and above the reflective faculties teaches the proper use of Imitation; to copy what is good and above all the prominent features of our Lord's character, charity and universal love.

28. Caution.

Caution tends naturally to circumspection, and it produces a cautious and considerate disposition of mind; persons so organized are continually on their guard, they look forward from fear of what may happen and are anxious to anticipate every occurence, they ask advice, take opinions and are still undecided; thus it produces doubt, irresolution, and wavering, which prevents vigorous and decisive conduct: when the organ is deficient in mature age, the individual is rash and precipitate, never apprehensive of the results of his conduct and thus he adopts rash resolutions and enters on hazardous enterprizes without foreseeing what must necessarily follow: to a due influence of this faculty we may trace the moral virtue that regulates the impulses of passion—looks to the future, and keeps the end of all things steadily in view. In ABUSE the faculty occasions fear and anxiety of the future, timid and desponding sentiments; no reliance upon Providence, too much thought about the morrow, forgetting that "sufficient for the day is the evil thereof"—Let a wise man, "Fear God and have no other fear," for this will lead him to be cautious against offences against Him, and if a man keeps this steadily in view, he will never violate the laws of man.

29. Temperance.

Temperance is allied to caution, it is to the animal portion of man what *caution* is to the intellectual: its existence is identified with the preceding organ by many phrenologists, and probably the developement of that organ, as it is closer too, and more active upon the animal passions may be coincident with this. In this way Temperance tends to *present* as cautiousness to *future* prudence, it gives mind the mastery over matter, overcomes Combativeness and the lower feelings, and teaches temperance in all things: carried into an erroneous action it produces meanness and almost avariciousness; the wise man whose animal nature predominates will learn the difference between *use*, and *abuse*, by exercising Temperance not by the abuse of the goodness and gifts of his Creator.

30. Conscientiousness.

Located between Cautiousness and Firmness. This faculty produces a feeling of *duty*, a desire of *justice*, and a love of *truth*; it is the organ that leads men to do as they would be done unto, and is the most elevated principle of human action: the faculty does not determine what is just or unjust, but causes a desire to do whatever the reflective faculties determine to be right and becoming. It is a portion of the organization that cannot be too much cultivated, as it is of the highest importance in guiding and directing, regulating and controlling the actions of the other faculties: it leads to a conviction of individual error, and the truth when asserted by others: it influences the whole being to exercise prudence, temperance and fortitude, in opposition to the baser desires of the propensities; it tends to overcome the energy of passion, to regulate and direct the affections, to root out prejudice, and give the sense of moral rectitude, that supports an honest man under distress and affliction: when the sentiment is not well developed, the ideas of right and wrong are weak, and injustice if in accordance with interest or inclination easily committed; and when the lower propensities are active, an individual with this organ small, will call that *justice*, which a person differently organized would at once condemn; these are they of whom the apostles spoke, "Unto the pure all things are pure: but unto them that are defiled and unbelieving, there is nothing pure:" but even their mind and *conscience* is defiled: remorse and repentance spring from this faculty: it should however be exerted *before*, not *after* an action—neither should it descend into immoderate personal chastisement; for no punishment of the body can wash out sin from the soul; the sentiment will never be abused if it be directed to preserve the "conscience, void of offence."

31. Firmness.

Firmness, is a tendency to *persist* in conduct, opinion, and purpose: the immediate emotion is termed Resolution. The organ is situated at the posterior part of the coronal region, close upon the middle line. This faculty seems to bear no relation to external objects, its influence adds a particular quality to other manifestations: whatever may be the predominant pursuit it seems to give *perseverance* in that pursuit; it contributes greatly to the success of an individual in a particular object, as he keeps steadily in one course. A person without the faculty may manifest equal desire, but will, perhaps, try a dozen methods of success without following out any one, thus fortitude and patience are the results of this organization: when duly exercised, it gives stability of character; a person who is not led by the accident of the moment, but one who aims at perfection, and duly keeps to the high road to arrive there: when combined with conscientiousness it gives moral courage, supports the martyr at the stake, and enables a man to go on through evil report and good report without turning to the right hand or the left: without this endowment, the most splendid talents are thrown away, as they never reach the summit of what is good, because like Reuben, "unstable as water they cannot excel."—In Abuse this faculty leads to obstinacy, stubbornness, infatuation in evil courses, or a constant aim at what is good, without perseverance to arrive at it.

32. Ideality.

The operation of this faculty is beautifully described by Shakspeare;—

"The poet's eye in a fine frenzy rolling,
Doth glance from heaven to earth, from earth to heaven,
And as imagination bodies forth
The forms of things unknown, the poet's pen
Turns them to shapes, and gives to airy nothing
A local habitation and a name."

The organ is situated nearly on the temporal ridge of the frontal bone. Gall called it, *the organ of poetry*, because "in every kind of poetry the sentiments are exalted, the expressions warm; and there must be rapture, inspiration, what is commonly called imagination or fancy." It is this faculty that produces the aspiration after *perfection*, it aims at endowing every object with the highest degree of perfection which it is capable of assuming, and is thus very valuable to man in his progressive changes towards a more virtuous and perfect existence. It gives a peculiar tinge to other faculties, making them aspire to exquisiteness, thus giving an expansion to the mental powers, which carries onwards, forwards, and upwards, makes them aim to be happy and form schemes for its attainment: it gives a keener relish to other faculties, in short, its operation is intellectually ennobling. In ABUSE it produces a finical and sickly refinement, fanciful opinions, love of show more than utility; it leads to novel reading, extravagant notions, and this gives a fictitious and unsteady character, unfitted for the severer walks of life.

33. Wonder.

This organ is situated immediately above *Ideality*; and the faculty gives faith in spiritual agency, in what is beyond the sphere of human vision, and which nevertheless requires to be believed; it inspires a love of the marvellous, the wonderful, the grand; a seeking for extraordinary events even in the most unlikely concerns, and a tinging of common-place with the emotions of superstition and romance. In the end of man's tyranny, God prophesies through the mouth of Isaiah that "he will make all men drunk with the wine of astonishment." In ABUSE, this faculty leads into much error, it inspires a love of what is novel and marvellous, a tendency to believe in magic, witchcraft, and other unlawful and unchristian arts, and when uncontrolled by the higher sentiments, to the pursuit of occult subjects; when united with the moral sentiments and due perception and reflection, it searches deep into the truth, tests spiritual causes and prophecies by research and belief, considering that nothing is impossible to God and that His goodness is sufficient for all.

34. Faith or Veneration.

Situated in the middle of the coronal region of the brain; gives an innate disposition to religious truth; a veneration for things sacred; belief in the word of God, and hope in Christ Jesus; it is this innate principle that bids the savage bow down to stocks and stones, to graven idols, and the works of his own hands; it is this that inspires the missionaries of God's word, and leads others to bestow their wealth in furthering the good cause; and to pray for the time when the "knowledge of the Lord shall cover the earth, as the waters cover the sea;" when abused, this organ leads to superstition, an undue reverence for the *material* portion of Christianity, to the depreciation of the *spiritual*, thus producing fanaticism, fear, and mystery; this organ requires to be guided by conscientiousness, and the light of God's word, as the only true guide to religion, as composed of its elements, Faith, Hope and Charity.

35. Hope.

The organ of Hope lies on each side of Veneration; the mental faculty being altogether different from desire, led phrenologists to seek for a primitive organ, and thus the faculty has been identified with this portion of the brain. In well formed characters, this faculty leads to sanguine expectation in the goodness of God, it produces the blessed hope of everlasting life, the perfect love that casteth out fear, through hope and belief in Christ; it gives confidence in all undertakings commenced and carried on in a Christian spirit; it is the true staff of moral and religous courage, buoying up the soul amid the darkest terrors of distress or desolation. Hope supports Faith, and perfects Charity, since without it, the religion of man would be dark, gloomy, and desponding; in abuse, the faculty is directed to hopes of this world only; it creates too sanguine expectations, leading to disappointment that is often the bitter but wholesome fruit of experience; it often leads to vain and foolish speculations, and sometimes to want of exertion from a hope of good happening; "hope deferred maketh the heart sick." When in unity with faith, benevolence, and the higher sentiments, it is productive of *Theosophy*, the knowledge of God from his works of love, and by a warm hope of everlasting life, leads men to subdue the lusts of the flesh, to be humble in their own wisdom, and to hope for the accomplishment of the great promise, "to be heirs of glory, and joint heirs with Jesus Christ."

36. Benevolence.

Benevolence is the noblest sentiment that man is enabled fully to exercise: it is in the coronal bone, central and immediately before the fontanel, it produces the generous and forgiving Christian, and the faculty is always delighted in doing good, and in ministering to the happiness of others; it compassionates distress, communicating a warmth of generous feeling that overcomes acquisitiveness and selfishness: it disposes to mildness of disposition, general kindness, charity, sympathy and love; it is the foundation of Christian charity and tends to relieve the wants and necessities of others. The higher sentiment is that of charity to the weaknesses of others, and a due regard to their opinions and errors; if too freely exercised it becomes abused that is, it inclines to generous extravagance, and alms-giving without regard to necessity in the object; it may thus be used to effect injustice to others, and although one of the noblest virtues of the human character it is useless unless exercised in a right way: for as St. Paul says—"though I give all my goods to feed the poor, and my body to be burned, and have not *Charity*, it profiteth me nothing."

37. Self Esteem.

Self Esteem rightly exercised confers self respect, a due regard to rank or station, and induces confidence in one's own abilities; the organ is placed just at the top or crown of the head. When exercised in a right way, it imparts a degree of self-satisfaction, and enables us to apply our powers to the best advantage in whatever station we are placed; it leads to self esteem, so that the individual contemns every action that is base and unworthy of an exalted mind; it restrains from forming improper connections, and this too when the moral qualities are not sufficient. When the organ is too small, the individual is bashful, has no reliance on himself, and from rating his abilities too low, gets them rated less. When large, it produces egotism, pride, hauteur, and self conceit. Combined with good moral sentiments, it is a valuable organ. In ABUSE it tends to self-love, self-will, and uncharitableness; and towards others contempt, disdain, and tyranny; it is a mortal enemy to Christian love and peace.

38. Love of Approbation.

This faculty regards the opinion that other persons form of us: the organ is situated on each side of *Self esteem* about half an inch from the lambdoidal suture: it produces the desire of approbation, admiration, praise and fame: it renders us anxious to please those whose approval we esteem, and to excel in whatever pursuit our associates admire. If well balanced by conscientiousness and veneration, it seeks the approval of the Great Judge of all things, by becoming worthy of eternal life: a due endowment is indispensable to an amiable character. In ABUSE it tends to vanity, a thirst for praise and flattery, a dread of the world's opinion, and a too easy giving way to the ways of the world to obtain the applause of the worthless;—the faculty is cultivated by the system of rewards for merit offered in youth,—it is not often the abstract value of the object so much as the approbation of those who know us. This organ causes bashfulness or *Mauvaise Honte*, and produces the fear of doing wrong, which it often originates by over anxiety to do well; it requires to be closely watched, as it leads to *envy*, one of the most subtle and dangerous passions, that afflict man in his fallen state; it stirs up the animal propensities and the earthly affections, overcoming the superior sentiments; the man who endeavours to seek the applause of others should remember that his Redeemer said, "And whosoever of you be the chief, let him be the servant of all." The faculty requires to be cultivated and regulated by conscientiousness, guided by the understanding to seek the applause of the good, and influenced by the spirit to seek the applause that is all in all to the christian, "Well done thou good and faithful servant, enter thou into the joy of thy Lord."

39. Sophistry.

This organ, called by the French authors, "*Ottin*, Tete Philosophie,"—is situated on the top of the forehead above Comparison and causality, and gives an intense love of philosophy and metaphysical research: when well supported by the moral sentiments and perceptive faculties, it gives a great power of reasoning well, but if the perceptives are deficient, it gives a love of theory without sufficient regard to facts, so that the process of induction is lost sight of: its greatest abuse causes the light of wisdom, which is Truth, to be darkened by spiritual delusion or wilful perversion of revelation: or it produces intellectual sophistry, which tends to support party prejudices, and clothe error in the vestments of truth—actuated by the moral sentiments, this faculty produces the power of detecting sophistry in the arguments of another and teaches the christian to be as "subtle as the serpent, and as harmless as the dove."

40. Prophecy.

This organ lies between Conscientiousness, Hope, Caution and Wonder; it produces a desire to compare the past with the future and judge of what will be; it influences to a study of prophetic writings and as the organ is actuated by wonder, or a desire of truth, so is the prophet true or false; and as the animal or moral and spiritual creature prevails, so will the person be dangerous or useful. St. Paul tells us, "despise not prophesying."—and he calls it a gift and adds prophecy shall cease, but Charity and Love never faileth;—and again he exhorts us above all things to seek to prophecy, which in the greek text signifies "*to teach the truth,*" and thus it tends to perfect Christian peace and establishes for ever the eternal power of love; this faculty teaches us to perfect the faculties by pointing their evil tendency and looking forward to the teaching of the Divine spirit, to perfect what is out of unity in the threefold nature of man, as a physical, intellectual, and spiritual being: it teaches us to wait for the time when the Great Teacher Christ shall come as the Spirit of Truth and teach us all things. The abuse of this faculty makes men become false prophets and teachers; history affords abundant instances of men acting under diseased organs who have thus become deluding fanatics. The humble Christian who follows his anointed master will strive to overcome all that is vicious, so that he may be able to inherit all things, and understand the great truth that "the testimony of Christ Jesus is the spirit of prophecy."

CONCLUSION.

This little work having extended to a greater length than was originally intended, it is purposed to continue the subject in another volume of similar size, to which this is the text book.—In that work we design to point out the influence of the organs in combination,—the harmony of Scripture with Phrenology—and a text book for perfecting the organization by means of Holy writ—our object in so doing, is to make Christians the *true* Phrenologists, and to make this science one of the great army of TRUTHS, now advancing to the battle of Armageddon. Our aim in this volume has been simply to point out the uses of Phrenology, and the truths whereon it is founded; in the next we purpose to consider the means, whereby the pious and humble reader of Scripture may be enabled to perfect his organization, so as to overcome the world,—to fight the good fight,—and indeed to be born again.

THE END.

PHRENOLOGY.

Public attention is solicited to this Science as practised on Christian principles, by

Mr. BUNNEY, 62, REGENT'S QUADRANT.

Phrenology is emphatically the Science of Mind; and it enables persons to ascertain what points of their character are defective without being deceived by self-love or flattery, because, the Brain being the agent through which the mind operates, acts as an index to the general state of the mind at any particular period: and since *Unhappiness—Ill success in life—Monomania—Nervousness—Erroneous or Evil Actions*—are all the results of mis-directed mental energy—so Phrenology is, under Divine Providence, the means of detecting those slight wanderings of the intellectual faculties into particular channels, which frequently terminate in permanent estrangement, or lasting mental misery and discontent. *Phrenological Advice,* as practised by Mr. Bunney, is an examination of the state of the mind, through its agent the brain, and a recommendation of those pursuits which are calculated to restore a disarranged unity or an unequal balance among the organs or dispositions of the mind.

Mr. Bunney having examined many thousand heads during the last ten years, and witnessed the very great success attending Phrenological advice when rightly administered and properly followed, desires to announce that he is at home from Ten till Five daily, at his Lecture Room, 62, Regent's Quadrant, where he will be happy to examine and advise persons as his long experience in accordance with the Holy Scriptures may render necessary. Mr. B. is well aware that many persons are deterred from visiting him by pecuniary reasons, but he begs to add that his invitation is for public good only, and that he expects no remuneration unless it is perfectly agreeable to the wishes and circumstances of the inquirer. Having examined one-half the members of our leading Universities, Oxford and Cambridge with valuable results to the parties themselves, Mr. B. must consider any further comment unnecessary.

Lector House believes that a society develops through a two-fold approach of continuous learning and adaptation, which is derived from the study of classic literary works spread across the historic timeline of literature records. Therefore, we aim at reviving, repairing and redeveloping all those inaccessible or damaged but historically as well as culturally important literature across subjects so that the future generations may have an opportunity to study and learn from past works to embark upon a journey of creating a better future.

This book is a result of an effort made by Lector House towards making a contribution to the preservation and repair of original ancient works which might hold historical significance to the approach of continuous learning across subjects.

HAPPY READING & LEARNING!

LECTOR HOUSE
LECTOR HOUSE LLP
E-MAIL: lectorpublishing@gmail.com

9 789356 140011

www.ingramcontent.com/pod-product-compliance
Lightning Source LLC
Chambersburg PA
CBHW031353230926
51848CB00002B/507
9789356140011